Did Y...

SUT...
AND CHEAM

A MISCELLANY

Compiled by Julia Skinner

With particular reference to the work of Martin Andrew and Keith Howell

THE FRANCIS FRITH COLLECTION

www.francisfrith.com

First published in the United Kingdom in 2006 by The Francis Frith Collection®

This edition published exclusively for Oakridge in 2010 ISBN 978-1-84589-525-9

British Library Cataloguing in Publication Data

Did You Know? Sutton and Cheam - A Miscellany
Compiled by Julia Skinner
With particular reference to the work of Martin Andrew and Keith Howell

The Francis Frith Collection
Frith's Barn, Teffont,
Salisbury, Wiltshire SP3 5QP
Tel: +44 (0) 1722 716 376
Email: info@francisfrith.co.uk
www.francisfrith.com

Printed and bound in Malaysia

Front Cover: **SUTTON, HIGH STREET 1932** 85078p

The colour-tinting is for illustrative purposes only, and is not intended to be historically accurate

CONTENTS

INTRODUCTION

In 1801 the population of Cheam numbered 616 people. By the 1911 census the figure for Cheam had risen to 6,200, and by that date Sutton was home to over 21,000 people, largely owing to its role as a major coaching centre on the main London to Brighton road. In the 19th century, as both towns grew, they rapidly lost their old weatherboarded cottages which were replaced by Victorian terraces of shops with first-storey flats. The suburbs grew quickly with the establishment of essential services; the key to this development was the founding of the Sutton Gas Company in 1857, and the provision of piped water and mains drainage by the Sutton Water Company, which was founded in 1864.

It was in the opening decades of the 20th century that both Sutton and Cheam underwent their most spectacular expansion. Improved railway connections to London and the desirability of life away from the noise and pollution of the rapidly expanding conurbation made this district a prime target for developers and new residents. In Sutton the suburbs of the late 19th and early 20th centuries each had a distinctive character: while East Sutton had something of an artisan flavour, the tree-lined and spacious development of Benhilton was considered to be the most superior area, and photograph 51193, opposite, shows a typical example of the grand villas that were built along Benhill Wood Road. It is unfortunate that large numbers of these houses have now gone, for from the 1950s onwards Sutton's commuter-land developers saw flats as the future. The large Victorian and Edwardian houses in spacious grounds were replaced by blocks of mostly three-storey flats. In some roads very few older houses survived, and in the case of Christchurch Park not one house survived the tide of flat building. Many of the older buildings in the town centre were also replaced in the 1960s and 1970s, such as the Municipal Offices, the Cock Hotel, the Greyhound, the Congregational Church, Shinner's department store, Len's of Sutton and much else besides, and new roads around the town opened up further sites for development, often with tower office blocks. However, Sutton remains a vibrant, successful town, and its pedestrianised High Street makes it a pleasant place to explore.

Up until the early 1920s, development in Cheam had been limited by the estates of Cheam Park on the west and Cheam Manor on the east, and the area still retained the appearance and feel of a country village. But then the Cheam House estate, Cheam Court Farm and the old brewery at the crossroads came on the market, leading to the creation of much of the village centre as it is today. Southwards, large detached urban houses occupied much of what had been downland, while the opening of the Sutton bypass in 1927 and the widening of the east-west road linking Croydon and Epsom encouraged the growth of motor traffic through the areas. By the start of the Second World War, much of the centre of Cheam had been redeveloped to cater for an ever-growing population; however, the developers managed to retain a great deal of Cheam's appealing character, and much of the charm of the town that is captured in the photographs in this book is still preserved today.

Sutton and Cheam were formerly in Surrey, but in 1965 the London Borough of Sutton was formed. As well as Sutton and Cheam, the Borough includes Beddington, Carshalton, and Wallington. The story of this area is full of fascinating characters and events, of which this book can only provide a brief glimpse.

SUTTON, BENHILTON, THE HILTON 1904 51193

3

SURREY DIALECT WORDS AND PHRASES

'Horny bug' - a stag beetle.

'Bodger' - a stick or tool used to make a hole in the ground for planting seeds.

'Vairn' - fern.

'Apern' - apron.

'Chart' - is a dialect word of Surrey and Kent. It comes from the Anglo-Saxon word 'ceart', meaning a rough common overgrown with gorse or bracken.

'Shick-shacks' - a name for oak-apples. Oak-Apple Day (29 May) was known as *'Shick-Shack Day'* in Surrey. 29 May was the birthday of Charles II, and this day celebrated the restoration of the monarchy in 1660.

The phrase *'using Ockham's razor'* (sometimes spelled Occam's) comes from the Surrey town of Ockham, between Dorking and Woking. William of Ockham (1270-1347) was a philosopher, theologian and Franciscan friar who developed the theory known as 'Ockham's Razor'. Ockham's view was that when there are several competing theories to explain a phenomenon, the simpler theory is usually the most likely. The 'razor' of the name of the theory alludes to the idea of something cutting away unnecessary assumptions.

An old rhyme about the area says:

> *Sutton for good mutton,*
> *Cheam for juicy beef,*
> *Croydon for a pretty girl,*
> *And Mitcham for a thief.*

LOCAL AVIATION HISTORY

The Roundshaw housing estate at Wallington was built on the site of the former Croydon Airport, which was created during the First World War to provide London with protection against attack by Zeppelins. The airport also played its part in the defence of London during the Second World War, with Hurricanes and Spitfires leaving from here to do battle in the skies. It became Britain's chief international airport in 1920, and throughout the inter-war years was virtually the only airport handling international traffic; Imperial Airways, which concentrated on developing long-distance overseas routes, was based initially at Croydon Airport.

The airport eventually became too small to cope with the increasing volume of air traffic, and the last passenger flight left Croydon Airport on 30 October 1959; the airport terminal has now been restored, and the Croydon Airport Visitor Centre was opened in October 2000 to tell the story of those golden days of commercial aviation.

Many of the world's pioneer aviators used the airport in its heyday in the 1920s and 1930s. One of these was the Australian navigator 'Bert' Hinkler, who made the first solo flight from Britain to Australia in 1928. He set off on his historic journey from Croydon Airport on 7 February, and landed in Darwin on 22 February, after flying his two-seat Avro 581E Avian biplane over 11,250 miles in fifteen and a half days. One of the exhibits in the Croydon Airport Visitor Centre is the flight bag of Britain's pioneering aviation heroine Amy Johnson. She became the first female pilot to fly solo from Britain to Australia, at the age of 26, in 1930. She began the historic flight in her de Havilland DH60 Gipsy Moth G-AAAH from Croydon Airport on 5 May 1930. She landed at Port Darwin, on the northern tip of Australia, nineteen days later, after a dangerous and eventful trip. Amy became a national heroine, and thousands of people came to cheer her on her arrival back at Croydon. A reporter on the Wallington and Carshalton Times wrote: 'Visitors to London have made a special journey to Croydon. Northern dialects mingle with the Cockney accent. And, of course, Croydonians are assembling in their hundreds accompanied by large contingents from Purley, Wallington, Carshalton, Sutton and Cheam … the public enclosure at Plough Lane is filled with thousands of people, all struggling for a good view-point. In Sandy Lane and Foresters Row there are 4,000 cars parked, while the whole length of the Purley Way is filled with humans all cheerfully facing a three-hour wait for their heroine'.

SUTTON AND CHEAM MISCELLANY

Archaeological finds from the Sutton area go back over 10,000 years, but the first real substantial evidence of habitation came with the excavation of a Roman villa at Beddington. There have also been finds of burials, coins and artefacts in various parts of the locality. Stonecot Hill and London Road, the A24, run along the course of what is now referred to as Stane Street, the Roman road which ran between London and Chichester. Coldharbour Lane in Beddington is also believed to have been a minor road in Roman times. These ancient roads formed part of the parish boundaries, which were established in the Anglo-Saxon period, the north boundary of Sutton following Stane Street, and the east boundary of Beddington parish following Coldharbour Lane.

Sutton and Cheam have been in the London Borough of Sutton since 1965, but were formerly in the county of Surrey. Surrey was never an independent kingdom in Anglo-Saxon times - the area was settled by the Middle Saxons, who left their name in the old name of Middlesex. Their territory seems to have crossed the River Thames to include Surrey, or Suthrie, the southern region or area. Surrey appears to have been variously controlled by the powerful Anglo-Saxon kingdoms of Mercia and Wessex before finally being absorbed into Wessex after AD825, when King Egbert finally defeated Beornwulf of Mercia. The names of both Sutton and Cheam first appear in a charter of Chertsey Abbey, which appears to be a 13th-century copy and enlargement of one which is dated AD727, but was probably drawn up 50 years before. In this charter, the name of Sutton is given as 'Suthtone' and Cheam is 'Cegeham'. The charter lists lands given to Chertsey Abbey by one Frithwald, a sub-regulus or 'under-king' of Surrey.

SUTTON, HIGH STREET c1965 S233103

SUTTON, ST NICHOLAS'S CHURCH 1932 85081

Chertsey Abbey was one of the richest and most powerful abbeys in England during the Middle Ages. The great Benedictine abbey was founded in AD666, refounded after Danish destruction around AD950, and rebuilt after 1110. Chertsey Abbey held the manor of Sutton until its dissolution in 1537, when it was taken over by Henry VIII who granted it to the Carews of Beddington. After various changes of ownership, the lordship of the manor was bought by Thomas Alcock in 1845. He sold part of the land for redevelopment, but also helped fund the fine new church of All Saints, Benhilton, built 1863-66 (see photograph B67002, below), and the total rebuilding of Sutton's parish church of St Nicholas, in 1862-64 (see photograph 85081 on page 7). In 1912 the lordship was stripped of manorial rights, and sold to the Lamplugh family. Chertsey Abbey itself virtually disappeared after its dissolution - its stone was reused by the king's masons at Nonsuch and Hampton Court palaces after 1538.

BENHILTON, ALL SAINTS' CHURCH c1955 B67002

SUTTON, THE COCK HOTEL 1890 27423a

Until the middle of the 18th century, Sutton was of no greater size than any of the other local villages. The first catalyst for growth was the turnpiking of the London to Brighton road, which went through Sutton, in 1755. Although after 1809 the route moved east to go through Croydon, in the 1840s around twenty coaches a day still changed horses at the Cock Hotel in the High Street. An east-west turnpike road which ran from Epsom to Croydon also passed through Sutton on the Carshalton and Cheam Roads, thus producing a major crossroads where development grew. There were toll-gates by the crossroads for both routes until 1863, when they were relocated: one to the Gander Green Lane junction on Cheam Road, the other further south on Brighton Road. The tolls were abolished in 1882.

Photograph 27423a on page 9 superbly captures the character of old Sutton at its central crossroads, and shows the old Cock Hotel, which sports a Cycle Touring Club badge, and a hanging sign on a beam spanning the road. Beyond the hotel, towards the station, there is still a large tree and a rural atmosphere. In the foreground there was once a toll-gate, which was only removed

SUTTON, THE COCK HOTEL 1898 41708

in 1882, eight years before the photograph was taken. To the left of the photograph is the old beer-house, known as the Cock Hotel Tap, which was replaced in 1896-98 with the spanking modern hotel seen in photograph 41708, below. The old hotel, seen in the background of 41708, was demolished soon after 1898.

SUTTON, HIGH STREET 1932 85078

A delightful period view of Sutton's High Street is shown in photograph 85078, above. An Austin 7 is just passing the Greyhound Hotel, on the right of the view. The Greyhound was one of Sutton's oldest inns, although it was rebuilt in 1873. Like the Cock Hotel, its signboard was carried on a beam across the road, which was removed in 1938. The Greyhound was demolished in 1959 and replaced by a Woolworth's store, which has now been relocated. The landmark tree in the pavement outside the Greyhound (also seen in photograph S233121 on page 43) survived until the storms of 1987.

The main road from Sutton to London originally climbed Angel Hill's ridge, but in the early 19th century a cutting was made. According to local legend this was created at the order of the Prince Regent, who used the London to Brighton road to travel to his Pavilion by the sea at Brighton. Other sources say the cutting was made in the 1770s as part of the turnpiking of the main road. Whichever version is true, the cutting remains at its original width, and photograph 34064, below, shows the elegant Victorian bridge that once crossed the main road. By 1937 the old bridge had become dangerous and was removed. It was replaced by a temporary steel structure, which was hit by German bombs in September 1940. A second steel girder bridge was erected; although it was intended to be temporary, it survived until about 1980, when the present concrete span, which is carried on imitation rubble stone abutments, was erected.

SUTTON, BENHILTON BRIDGE 1894 34064

The London parishes were able to send their paupers into the countryside in Victorian times by building vast edifices to house them far away from London. Photograph 38943, opposite, shows one such establishment, the South Metropolitan District School; the first school building was erected at Sutton in the 1850s for both boys and girls, but a separate school for girls was built later, on the Banstead Road. The school could house 1,500 vagrant and pauper children. Boys were taught a trade, mainly various building and construction skills, shoemaking, tailoring, painting, plumbing, baking or gardening and farm work, and the girls were mainly trained to become domestic servants. The school closed in 1902 and the buildings were later used as a hospital and asylum, a workhouse and a First World War prisoner of war camp. In 1946 the majority of the school became Belmont Hospital, but most of the hospital buildings were finally demolished in 1982 and the site was used for the Belmont housing estate; part of the site of the girls' school on the Banstead Road was taken over by the Royal Marsden Hospital in 1962, which specialises in cancer treatment.

Photograph 50284, opposite, shows Sutton's Public Baths, which were around the corner from where Throwley Road (now Throwley Way) once turned to the north. In the background is the chimney for the boiler house which was used to heat the pool water and the slipper baths. The Public Baths building was demolished in 1971.

The Angel Hotel is situated at the top of Angel Hill, where once horses were changed before journeying down into Sutton. The early 19th-century inn had a livery and bait stables attached. The term 'livery stables' meant that a customer's own horse could be kept there until required, on a weekly or monthly rate. 'Bait stables' offered the service of keeping a customer's horse while he visited nearby; the horse would meanwhile be watered and fed - the Victorian equivalent of a car park.

SUTTON, THE SOUTH METROPOLITAN DISTRICT SCHOOL 1896 38943

SUTTON, THE PUBLIC BATHS 1903 50284

SUTTON, THE COCK HOTEL AND HIGH STREET c1955 S233029

The centre of Sutton has been constantly demolished and rebuilt, especially in and near the High Street. Photograph S233029, above, shows the Cock Hotel of 1896-98 (right of photograph), on the corner of Carshalton Road, and its sign, topped by a cockerel, in the middle of the road. The Cock Hotel was demolished in 1961 and replaced by an office block called Old Inn House. The premises of William Pile's bookshop and stationers (the white building to the left of the Cock Hotel) was built in 1882; William Pile's establishment closed in 1966, but the building survived for some years before being demolished in 1983 and replaced with a four-storey red brick office building that now houses Lloyds TSB. Another casualty of the demolition gangs was the Municipal Offices, whose top tower is conspicuous further down the High Street; this building, also shown in photograph 48864 on page 45, was demolished in 1971 and replaced by the concrete Surrey House facing the High Street.

Photograph S233096, opposite, of Sutton's High Street was probably taken from the roof of the Cock Hotel. In the middle distance on the left is the large cornice and parapet of Shinner's department store. Ernest Shinner opened his first shop in 1899, and the business rapidly expanded to take over the whole terrace. In 1934 Ernest Shinner bought the Baptist church at the corner of Hill Road. This he demolished, and the classical façade of his store was completed. In the 1980s Shinner's was taken over by Allders of Croydon; the building was demolished in 1992.

SUTTON, HIGH STREET c1960 S233096

SUTTON, THE WESLEYAN CHURCH 1913 65223

This photograph shows the sumptuous building of Sutton's Wesleyan Church. It is distinguished by its fine tower and unusual spire, which is based on the 'crown' of the 15th-century tower of St Giles's Cathedral, Edinburgh. The spire is carried on four converging flying buttresses.

SUTTON, THE GREEN 1898 41713

The road to London from Sutton passes through The Green, an attractive open area which was preserved by the 1810 Act of Parliament that enclosed the rest of the former common land for agriculture. The Green once included a pond, but this was notorious for its summer stinks; in 1894 a new concrete base and side walls were completed in an effort to alleviate the problem and tidy up the area. Photograph 41713, above, shows the pond a few years later, in its heyday. The pond was known as Victoria Pond because the weeping willow on its island was planted in 1838 to commemorate Queen Victoria's coronation. An elm was planted in 1898 to commemorate her diamond jubilee. In 1955 the pond was filled in, and is now only a memory.

The Swan Bar of the Greyhound Hotel at Carshalton is said to be haunted by the ghost of a 19th-century traveller who froze to death on the doorstep.

Gander Green Lane, shown in photograph 41716, below, formed the old boundary parish between Sutton and Cheam. This view, looking north, shows the small roadside pond which existed on the east side of the road, midway between the S-bend and what is now West Sutton Railway Station.

SUTTON, GANDER GREEN LANE 1898 41716

CHEAM, ST DUNSTAN'S CHURCH
AND THE WAR MEMORIAL 1925 77067a

The origins of human settlement at Cheam date back at least 2,000 years: the remains of hut circles were still visible until recently on Banstead Downs, and examples of early British and Roman coins were discovered in the area during the opening decades of the 20th century.

In old documents, Cheam has been spelt in around fourteen different ways, including Cheiham, Kaham, Keyham and Cheiham, and it is recorded in the Domesday Book of 1086 as Ceiham. It is believed that at the time of the Domesday survey there were around 300 inhabitants and some 50 houses in Cheam.

Before 1018, Cheam was held by the Abbot and Convent of Chertsey, but was then given by the Anglo-Saxon King Athelstan to the monks of Christ Church, Canterbury - they issued the warning that anyone who infringed their rights would be excommunicated. After the Norman Conquest, Archbishop Lanfranc divided Cheam into two manors, East and West Cheam, keeping the former himself and allotting the other to the monks.

In the later Middle Ages the Cheam area was known for its potteries, producing what is known as Cheam whiteware, a type of wheelthrown pottery which is frequently found on archaeological sites in London. The local potters appear to have specialised in making jugs, and although the pottery is known as whiteware because it was made from a white-firing clay, it was actually produced in various shades of buff, often with a green glaze. Two medieval pottery kilns have been discovered so far in Cheam, one in Parkside, which dates from the 14th century, and the other in the High Street, which dates from c1500. Examples of Cheam pottery can be seen in Whitehall on Malden Road.

CHEAM PARK HOUSE 1928 81435

In 1539, Archbishop Cranmer exchanged the manor of East Cheam with Henry VIII for Chislet Park in Kent, and on the Dissolution of the Monasteries the king also took possession of West Cheam manor. In 1537 Henry purchased the village, church and estate of neighbouring Cuddington parish from Sir Richard Codington and, having demolished the buildings there, embarked on his plan to build the magnificent palace of Nonsuch, using a Florentine architect. The palace was still half-finished at the time of the king's death in 1547, but even so, both he and his daughter, Elizabeth I, spent much time here. Cheam acquired great importance from its proximity to the palace of Nonsuch, an association that continued beyond Elizabeth's reign, for it was visited by both James I and Charles I.

The building shown in photograph 79471, below, is not the original great Tudor palace of 'None such' built by Henry VIII, which was subsequently given by Charles II to his mistress, Lady Castlemaine. She, being in debt, pulled the palace down, sold the contents and materials for building purposes, and turned the park into farmland. The land was eventually bought in 1797 by Samuel Farmer, who built this two-storey, castellated house in 1802-05. It stands further east and closer to Cheam than the original Tudor palace. The asymmetrical frontage of the new 'palace' was designed by Jeffry Wyattville, who later went on to work on the reconstruction of Windsor Castle (for which he was knighted). The building was further augmented in 1845.

CHEAM, NONSUCH PARK PALACE 1927 79471

NORTH CHEAM, LONDON ROAD c1955 N258045

The lonely ghost of a tall man dressed in a long black cloak is said to stand by the main eastern gate into Nonsuch Park. The story goes that he was once the sweetheart of an adulterous young woman who was murdered in the park by her jealous husband when he found out about her indiscretions.

Photograph N258045, above, shows the shopping parade on London Road in North Cheam. At the far end of the parade is the prominent sign for the Granada cinema, which seated 2,000 people. The cinema had a Wurlitzer organ which was played during the intervals to entertain the customers, and its patrons were promised that they would breath air which had been 'laundered in a synthetic mountain stream'.

Photograph 51199, below, shows the playground at the rear of the Cheam School buildings in 1904 - the site is now occupied by Tabor Court alongside the present bypass. The tree on the left of the photograph still stands in the garage yard of Tabor Court. The school was initially installed at Whitehall on Malden Road in the year of the Great Plague of London in 1665, and moved to this site in 1719. One of the pupils of Cheam School was Prince Philip, Duke of Edinburgh. The school moved again, to Berkshire, in 1934, but the fine school chapel remains today in Dallas Road as St Christopher's Roman Catholic Church.

CHEAM, THE SCHOOL 1904 51199

CHEAM, WHITEHALL 1925 77064

CHEAM, PARK LANE 1925 77062

CHEAM, CHEAM PARK HOUSE LODGE 1938 88279

The timber-framed jettied house called Whitehall standing on the corner of Park Lane and Malden Road in Cheam, seen on the left of photograph 77064 on pages 28-29, is thought to have been built as a farmhouse c1500, and over the centuries it has undergone numerous alterations and additions. It was acquired and restored by the local borough council in 1963, and is now open to the public. This photograph also shows Laurel Cottage and Vault Cottage along the Maldon Road, with the elegant rectory beyond, which in its earliest parts dates back to 1575. According to tradition, an undercroft existed behind these cottages where the first pupils of Cheam School assembled to escape the ravages of the plague in London in 1665. The area was covered in during the 1930s.

The picturesque and simple weatherboarded cottages shown in photograph 77062, opposite above, were once among many in the village; they were originally built for workers on the Nonsuch estate.

The building at the foot of Park Lane shown in photograph 88279, opposite below, with its stuccoed walls, pedimented porch and ornamental iron gates, was built around 1820 as the lodge to Cheam Park House (shown in photograph 81435 on page 24); that edifice failed to survive the Second World War, having been wrecked by a V1 flying bomb in July 1944. Its owners then gave the park to the borough council. The lodge is still standing, although in a sadly dilapidated condition.

CHEAM, ST DUNSTAN'S CHURCH AND THE LYCHGATE 1925 77068

St Dunstan's Church in Cheam (see photograph 77068, above) was built in 1862-64 by G A Pownall in florid French Gothic style; the broach spire of the church with its lancet windows was added to the original structure in 1870. Pownall's church was built alongside the old medieval church, which was largely demolished when the new building was completed. Only the east window and chancel were preserved as the Lumley Chapel (see opposite).

Photograph 27586, below, shows some of the numerous monuments housed within the Lumley Chapel, which once formed a part of Cheam's old medieval church. The carved alabaster tomb of the first Lady Lumley, who died in 1592, dominates this view of the chapel's south side. She was the daughter of Henry Fitzalan, the 18th Earl of Arundel, and is depicted on the panel above the tomb's marble top, kneeling at prayer. The two front panels show her three children, with the family's coat of arms emblazoned on the damaged end panel. On the extreme left of the photograph is the carved memorial to James Bovey and his wife; he was probably connected to Cheam School, and died in 1695.

CHEAM, ST DUNSTAN'S CHURCH, THE LUMLEY CHAPEL 1890 27586

33

CHEAM, THE BROADWAY 1932 85087

The timber-framed cottage shown in photograph 77066, opposite, originally occupied a site in Maldon Road in Cheam (now the Broadway), closer to the main crossroads, but it stood in the way of the widening of the street. In 1922 the cottage was completely dismantled and re-erected further north; regrettably its original 'rye dough' infilling (clay mixed with rye straw) was replaced with Portland cement. The cottage is now used as a shop. It can be see again in its new location behind the tree on the left of photograph 85087 on pages 34-35.

In the 19th and early 20th centuries many acres of lavender were grown around Cheam and Sutton Common, supplying the distilling industry focused around Mitcham. The lavender harvest took place in late July and August, when the oil content of the flowers was at its highest, and was cut by hand by a labour force of men, women and children using small sickles. Some of the people who helped with the lavender harvest came from Ireland, and would then move on to Kent to help with the hop picking. The English lavender industry declined in the early 20th century when cheaper supplies of French lavender came on to the market.

CHEAM, THE OLD COTTAGE 1925 77066

CHEAM, HIGH STREET 1925 77051

CHEAM, EWELL ROAD 1932 85088

The name of Cheam came to national prominence when in November 1954 the scriptwriters Ray Galton and Alan Simpson launched their classic comedy creation 'Hancock's Half Hour' on BBC Radio. Featuring its eponymous and bombastic hero Anthony Aloysius St John Hancock and assorted companions, it was set at what has become one of the best-known of all fictional addresses: 23 Railway Cuttings, East Cheam. Over the course of 36 episodes of the now venerated radio and television shows, the events at Hancock's mythical residence entertained audiences until December 1959. However, Hancock's address had more than a hint of historical basis in fact. When the branch railway line from Sutton to Wimbledon was constructed in 1928, it had necessitated the excavation of a substantial amount of soil to create the cutting that carries the line to West Sutton Station (the spoil was used to fill in old chalk pits, which extended the grounds of Sutton Cricket Club). So, in theory, Hancock's legendary residence should have been positioned somewhere in the vicinity of Western Road; Messrs Galton and Simpson came perilously close to giving their fictional creation a real address.

The London Borough of Sutton is known as 'The Greener Borough' because of its commitment to eco-friendly policies. The Borough recycles more waste than any other London borough, and has a target to recycle 50% of all household waste. There are also more trees in the Borough of Sutton than any other London borough, as well as more than 1,000 acres of open space.

SPORTING SUTTON AND CHEAM

Sutton United FC has had a number of significant football personalities connected with it. Both Jimmy Hill and Malcolm Allison (later manager of Manchester City) coached the team, and Dario Gradi played for Sutton United before making his name as manager of Crewe Alexander for over 20 years.

The record attendance at Sutton United FC is 14,000. This was for an FA Cup tie against Leeds United in January 1970. The Leeds side at that time was one of the best in the country, including eleven full internationals, and Leeds won the game 6-0.

Another notable FA Cup game at Gander Green was Sutton United's famous victory over Coventry City in 1989. This was the last occasion on which a non-League team beat a team from the top division. Interestingly, it is thought that the gap between the two clubs in League positions (Coventry were 6th in Division 1 at the time) makes it the biggest FA Cup upset of all time.

One of the best-known footballers to come from the area is the goalkeeper Neil Sullivan, born in Sutton in 1970. Sullivan has had a long and distinguished career with Wimbledon, Tottenham, Chelsea and Leeds, and was also eligible to play for Scotland, for whom he was selected 28 times.

David Morgan (1933-2004) was a fine club cricketer for Cheam Cricket Club. Morgan represented the club for many years, taking over 1,300 wickets in the Surrey League, and playing in the National Club final at Lords at the age of 57. Bill Frindall, the famous cricket statistician, has claimed that Morgan was possibly the best bowler never to have played first-class cricket.

Sutton Cricket Club has a distinguished history. Amongst other achievements, the club won the very first Surrey Championship in 1968. The club has had a large number of notable players, including Colin Cowdrey, South Africa Test Match star Graham Pollock, John Fry (the first man to score 10,000 runs in the Surrey League), and Maurice Jewell, later a captain of Worcestershire. The legendary WG Grace also appeared as a guest on occasions.

James Cracknell was born in Sutton in 1972. Along with Sir Stephen Redgrave, Matthew Pinsent and Tim Foster, he was part of Britain's successful rowing team which won a gold medal in the coxless fours at the Olympic Games in Sydney in 2000.

SUTTON, GENERAL VIEW c1965 S233136

QUIZ QUESTIONS

Answers on page 48.

1. Cheam's public library in Church Road stands on a site that was occupied by a field gun when the memorial gardens by the war memorial were opened following the First World War. What happened to the gun?

2. Where in Sutton can you find the original waiting room of Sutton's first station?

3. Who is Sutton's Secombe Theatre named after?

4. Where in the London Borough of Sutton can you find 'The Bug', and what is it?

5. What is the connection between the London Borough of Sutton and Hiawatha, the Native American hero of a poem by Longfellow?

6. What is the connection between Sutton and the recent successful film 'The War of the Worlds'?

7. Henry VIII is said to have begun the building of Nonsuch Palace to celebrate the birth of his son - what was the child's name?

8. Which British Prime Minister was born at St Helier Hospital, Carshalton, in 1943?

9. Which rock music supergroup performed their first official booking in Surrey at the Woodstock Hotel, North Cheam on 5 October 1962?

10. The centrepiece of Sutton's Millennium Garden in the Town Square is an Armillary Sphere - what is this?

SUTTON, HIGH STREET c1965 S233121

RECIPE

SUTTON APPLE PIE

Ingredients

450g/1lb cooking apples, peeled, cored and sliced
The juice and zest of half a small lemon
75g/3oz butter
2-3 tablespoonfuls orange marmalade

110g/4oz self-raising flour
50g/2oz soft light brown sugar
50g/2oz porridge oats
A further small amount of butter for cooking the oat and flour mixture, and for adding to the top of the pie

Pre-heat the oven to 190 degrees C/375 degrees F/Gas Mark 5.

Place the apples, lemon zest and juice in a saucepan, adding a small amount of water if necessary, and cook the apples gently until they are soft. Push the apple mixture through a sieve to form a purée, and stir in the marmalade.

Rub the 75g/3oz butter into the flour until the mixture resembles fine breadcrumbs, then stir in the sugar and oats. Melt a small amount of the extra butter in a frying pan and cook the oat and flour mixture over a low heat for about one minute, stirring all the time so that it does not burn.

Butter a shallow flan dish, divide the flour and oat mixture in half and press one half on to the base of the dish. Spread with the apple puree, and put the remainder of the flour and oat mixture on top. Sprinkle a little extra sugar on top, and dot with small pieces of butter. Bake for 30-40 minutes, and serve with custard or cream.

RECIPE

SYLLABUB

Syllabub was a popular dessert in Tudor times, and is just the sort of dish that would have been enjoyed in Nonsuch Palace.

Ingredients
150ml/5fl oz white wine
2 tablespoonfuls lemon juice
2 teaspoonfuls lemon zest
75g/3oz caster sugar
300ml/10fl oz double cream

Put the wine, lemon juice, zest and sugar into a bowl. Leave to stand for at least three hours. Add the cream and whip until the mixture stands in soft peaks. Transfer to 6 wine glasses or glass dishes and decorate with lemon zest.

Chill for several hours before serving.

RECIPE

WATERCRESS SOUP

The area around Carshalton and Beddington was once noted for its watercress beds - the name Carshalton is believed to mean 'cress-stream'.

Ingredients

50g/2oz butter

2 bunches of watercress with their stalks removed, washed and chopped

1 medium onion, chopped

25g/1oz plain flour

600ml/1 pint milk

450ml/¾ pint chicken or vegetable stock

6 tablespoonfuls single cream

Melt the butter in a large pan, and gently fry the watercress and onion for a few minutes until softened. Stir in the flour and cook for a further one minute. Slowly stir in the milk, and then the stock. Bring to the boil, stirring all the time, until thickened, then cover and simmer gently for 30 minutes.

Remove from heat and cool for a few minutes, then liquidise. Before serving, add the cream and reheat gently, taking care not to allow the soup to boil. Serve with a swirl of cream and a sprig of watercress leaves to garnish.

QUIZ ANSWERS

1. Local people felt that the gun's inclusion in this setting was highly inappropriate, particularly when it was identified as a captured German model, and one night some local youths removed it and tossed it into the sandpit at Cheam Brickworks.

2. The waiting room of the first railway station building at Sutton was a small timber structure, erected in 1847. In 1865 the waiting room was bought from the Brighton Railway Company by Sutton Cricket Club, and it was re-erected in the cricket ground at Cheam Road with a thatched roof and used as a pavilion until a new pavilion was erected in 1906 (this new pavilion was destroyed by bombing in the Second World War). The station building is still in the cricket club grounds, although it now has a tiled roof, and is used as a storeroom by the groundsman.

3. The Secombe Theatre is named after a famous resident, the late Sir Harry Secombe, actor, singer and member of 'The Goon Show', who used to live in Cheam Road. He was also president of the League of Friends of St Helier Hospital at Carshalton for almost 30 years. The second volume of Sir Harry's autobiography was titled 'Strawberries and Cheam'.

4. 'The Bug' is the name of the shelter in the Sutton Ecology Centre at Festival Walk, Carshalton. It was designed by Stephen Gittner and mostly built by volunteers. It is known as 'The Bug' because its curved shape resembles an insect.

5. The acclaimed black composer Samuel Coleridge-Taylor is buried at Bandon Hill Cemetery at Wallington; his best-known work is 'Hiawatha's Wedding'. He was born in Holborn in London in 1875, but was brought up in the Croydon area; his mother was English and his father was a doctor from Sierra Leone in West Africa. Samuel studied violin with a local musician and enrolled at the Royal College of Music as a violin student in 1890, but two years later he switched to composition, and soon began to make a name for himself. The turning point in his musical career came in 1898, when he was 23, when Sir Edward Elgar asked him to compose a piece for the Three Choirs Festival; this was his 'Ballade in A Minor', which was a critical and popular success. Samuel Coleridge-Taylor died tragically young, at the age of 37, from pneumonia.

6. The film of 'The War of the Worlds' was based on a novel written by H G Wells, who lived for a time in a semi-detached house at South Sutton.

7. The son of Henry VIII was Prince Edward (later Edward VI), whose mother was the king's third wife, Jane Seymour.

8. Sir John Major, who served as Prime Minister from 1990 to 1997.

9. The Rolling Stones.

10. An Armillery Sphere is a model of the universe. Armillery Spheres were particularly used in medieval times to study the movement of the planets and made astronomical calculations.

SUTTON, BENHILL ROAD 1903 50287

FRANCIS FRITH

PIONEER VICTORIAN PHOTOGRAPHER

Francis Frith, founder of the world-famous photographic archive, was a complex and multi-talented man. A devout Quaker and a highly successful Victorian businessman, he was philosophical by nature and pioneering in outlook. By 1855 he had already established a wholesale grocery business in Liverpool, and sold it for the astonishing sum of £200,000, which is the equivalent today of over £15,000,000. Now in his thirties, and captivated by the new science of photography, Frith set out on a series of pioneering journeys up the Nile and to the Near East.

INTRIGUE AND EXPLORATION

He was the first photographer to venture beyond the sixth cataract of the Nile. Africa was still the mysterious 'Dark Continent', and Stanley and Livingstone's historic meeting was a decade into the future. The conditions for picture taking confound belief. He laboured for hours in his wicker dark-room in the sweltering heat of the desert, while the volatile chemicals fizzed dangerously in their trays. Back in London he exhibited his photographs and was 'rapturously cheered' by members of the Royal Society. His reputation as a photographer was made overnight.

VENTURE OF A LIFE-TIME

By the 1870s the railways had threaded their way across the country, and Bank Holidays and half-day Saturdays had been made obligatory by Act of Parliament. All of a sudden the working man and his family were able to enjoy days out, take holidays, and see a little more of the world.

With typical business acumen, Francis Frith foresaw that these new tourists would enjoy having souvenirs to commemorate their days out. For the next thirty years he travelled the country by train and by pony and trap, producing fine photographs of seaside resorts and beauty spots that were keenly bought by millions of Victorians. These prints were painstakingly pasted into family albums and pored over during the dark nights of winter, rekindling precious memories of summer excursions. Frith's studio was soon supplying retail shops all over the country, and by 1890 F Frith & Co had become the greatest specialist photographic publishing company in the world, with over 2,000 sales outlets, and pioneered the picture postcard.

FRANCIS FRITH'S LEGACY

Francis Frith had died in 1898 at his villa in Cannes, his great project still growing. By 1970 the archive he created contained over a third of a million pictures showing 7,000 British towns and villages.

Frith's legacy to us today is of immense significance and value, for the magnificent archive of evocative photographs he created provides a unique record of change in the cities, towns and villages throughout Britain over a century and more. Frith and his fellow studio photographers revisited locations many times down the years to update their views, compiling for us an enthralling and colourful pageant of British life and character.

We are fortunate that Frith was dedicated to recording the minutiae of everyday life. For it is this sheer wealth of visual data, the painstaking chronicle of changes in dress, transport, street layouts, buildings, housing and landscape that captivates us so much today, offering us a powerful link with the past and with the lives of our ancestors.

Computers have now made it possible for Frith's many thousands of images to be accessed almost instantly. The archive offers every one of us an opportunity to examine the places where we and our families have lived and worked down the years. Its images, depicting our shared past, are now bringing pleasure and enlightenment to millions around the world a century and more after his death.

For further information visit: www.francisfrith.com

INTERIOR DECORATION

Frith's photographs can be seen framed and as giant wall murals in thousands of pubs, restaurants, hotels, banks, retail stores and other public buildings throughout Britain. These provide interesting and attractive décor, generating strong local interest and acting as a powerful reminder of gentler days in our increasingly busy and frenetic world.

FRITH PRODUCTS

All Frith photographs are available as prints and posters in a variety of different sizes and styles. In the UK we also offer a range of other gift and stationery products illustrated with Frith photographs, although many of these are not available for delivery outside the UK – see our website for more information on the products available for delivery in your country.

THE INTERNET

Over 100,000 photographs of Britain can be viewed and purchased on the Frith website. The website also includes memories and reminiscences contributed by our customers, who have personal knowledge of localities and of the people and properties depicted in Frith photographs. If you wish to learn more about a specific town or village you may find these reminiscences fascinating to browse. Why not add your own comments if you think they would be of interest to others? See **www.francisfrith.com**

PLEASE HELP US BRING FRITH'S PHOTOGRAPHS TO LIFE

Our authors do their best to recount the history of the places they write about. They give insights into how particular towns and villages developed, they describe the architecture of streets and buildings, and they discuss the lives of famous people who lived there. But however knowledgeable our authors are, the story they tell is necessarily incomplete.

Frith's photographs are so much more than plain historical documents. They are living proofs of the flow of human life down the generations. They show real people at real moments in history; and each of those people is the son or daughter of someone, the brother or sister, aunt or uncle, grandfather or grandmother of someone else. All of them lived, worked and played in the streets depicted in Frith's photographs.

We would be grateful if you would give us your insights into the places shown in our photographs: the streets and buildings, the shops, businesses and industries. Post your memories of life in those streets on the Frith website: what it was like growing up there, who ran the local shop and what shopping was like years ago; if your workplace is shown tell us about your working day and what the building is used for now. Read other visitors' memories and reconnect with your shared local history and heritage. With your help more and more Frith photographs can be brought to life, and vital memories preserved for posterity, and for the benefit of historians in the future.

Wherever possible, we will try to include some of your comments in future editions of our books. Moreover, if you spot errors in dates, titles or other facts, please let us know, because our archive records are not always completely accurate—they rely on 140 years of human endeavour and hand-compiled records. You can email us using the contact form on the website.

Thank you!

For further information, trade, or author enquiries
please contact us at the address below:

**The Francis Frith Collection, Frith's Barn, Teffont,
Salisbury, Wiltshire, England SP3 5QP.**
Tel: +44 (0)1722 716 376 Fax: +44 (0)1722 716 881
e-mail: sales@francisfrith.co.uk **www.francisfrith.com**